GOLF: THE LONG GAME

1   (overleaf) Tommy Horton driving

BATSFORD SPORTS BOOKS
General Editor: Robert Bateman

GOLF: THE LONG GAME

Tommy Horton

B. T. BATSFORD LTD LONDON

First published 1969
© Tommy Horton 1969

Filmset by Keyspools Ltd, Golborne, Lancashire,
and printed in Great Britain
by Fletcher and Son Ltd, Norwich
for the publishers
B. T. BATSFORD LTD
4 Fitzhardinge Street, London W1

7134 0316 0

Contents

Illustrations

Acknowledgment

The author and publishers would like to thank the following for permission to reproduce the illustrations which appear in this book:

The Press Association Ltd, for Plates 1, 10, 69.
United Press International (UK) Ltd, for Plate 4.
Barratts Photo Press Ltd, for Plate 5.
E. D. Lacey, for Plate 31.
Frank Gardner, for all Plates other than the above-named.

1 Think well—and play well!

The best club in the bag is a good temperament. That is a common saying in golf and one of the truest. All the world's best players have this in common: they all think positively. They all go out on to the course expecting the best and because of this, more often than not, they get it. Indeed at the top, where all players hit the ball well, it is very often temperament that separates the men from the boys. The ruthless touch is essential if one is to reach the heights in professional golf.

Although the accent isn't quite so strongly placed on the mental side in club golf, it is still of vital importance. The average club golfer will make two birdies and then go and take an eight or a nine. This is often because he is thinking badly. His mind is still on those lovely birdies instead of on the hole he is playing. Again, a club golfer will come to the 14th or 15th tee with a par finish needed for a good score. More often than not he will get excited and begin thinking about the last putt on the 18th when, in fact, he should be trying to concentrate on his drive from the 15th tee. Then his mind will wander to the clubhouse and he will picture himself making a victory speech. When these sort of thoughts cross your mind, it is usually the end of your good round.

It is essential to keep calm, right until the final putt is in the can. Then you can start preparing that victory speech. Neil Coles (2) is a man who has a marvellous temperament. He is able to divorce himself from pressure and the surroundings and concentrate on playing each shot. It seems ironical that Neil refuses to fly when he is so unruffled on the golf course.

As far as I am concerned, if I can keep calm and do everything slowly under pressure, then I do it correctly. When I was being sponsored by London businessman Mr Ernest Butten, he bought a book and said to each member of his squad: 'Open this book at page 84 and read the fifth line down.' This line said: 'When the pressure builds up, slow down.' I have always remembered that during my tournament days, and I hope I always will. It is the sort of slogan that can mean the difference between finishing first and second in a tournament. If you can slow down under pressure, and help your mind to think clearly, then you have a chance of playing your normal game when the chips are down.

I have often been guilty of letting the crowd at tournaments upset me during an important period of play. People don't often realise that when you are out there in a tournament you can hear almost everything the fans are saying. I often hear people talking, and now I just walk away from people if they speak to me during a round. After a round I am happy to talk to anyone, but I find it puts me off if I start holding conversations during play.

People are always coming up and telling me how other players are doing. I don't want to know how they are doing; I just like concentrating on my own game. In the 1968 RTV tournament in Ireland, which gave me my first

2   *Neil Coles, a man with a marvellous temperament for golf*

major win, I arrived at the 14th hole knowing that I was two shots ahead of my partner. Then someone in the crowd told me he was lying second. I just forgot all this and, in fact, began attacking the course more at the end than I did over the first few holes. I did this within reason, of course, concentrating like mad on all the shots to the green and the putts, because this is where a tournament is won or lost.

All golfers should learn that it is bad policy to listen to any talk of how the tournament is going until that final putt is down. If you do you can become very confused. Some people have lost events by trying to play too safe because they have overheard the wrong information in the crowd. Most players in a tournament ought to know whether they are doing well or not. They must trust their own judgment of the situation rather than listen to any old information which is often totally wrong.

Many club golfers begin their round not mentally prepared to play the opening hole. They arrive at the course late, dash to the locker room, change in a ghastly rush, and end up on the first tee in a terrible state. It is not surprising that the player who does this often starts with a card-wrecking eight. He just isn't in the right frame of mind to play golf after rushing.

Mental preparation is important to any golfer. In the Agfacolor tournament at Stoke Poges in 1968, I arrived late for one round because my alarm failed to go off. I went out and shot a disappointing score and the two or three strokes I dropped were almost entirely due to the rush I experienced before teeing off. I eventually ended up three strokes behind Clive Clark *(3)*, who won the

3 Clive Clark, winner of the 1968 Agfacolor event at Stoke Poges. If I had not arrived late for one of the rounds I might have challenged him for first place. In the end, I finished three strokes behind Clive

event. If I had organised myself better before starting in the first round, who knows what might have happened? I like to arrive at an event over an hour before I am due to go off. This gives me ample time to prepare myself for a round. The club golfer who wants to do well should try and follow a similar plan of action. If he does, he will be surprised how much better his golf will be.

For the professional, the session on the practice ground is a must. At big events like the Open or Ryder Cup, the practice grounds are always the centre of attraction for spectators, because they provide an opportunity to get really close to the stars.

The stars often respond to their close interest by joking with the crowds. The 1968 US Open champion, Lee Trevino (4), is a real favourite on the practice ground, and some of his jokes wouldn't be out of place at the Palladium! Dashing Doug Sanders, too, always attracts a crowd when he strides down to the practice ground dressed in his colour for the day. That can be anything from bright red to dark blue or lime green. Arnold Palmer is yet another man who attracts crowds like a magnet when he steps on to the practice ground. I have often heard people say that they enjoyed watching the stars on the practice ground as much as playing in the tournament proper.

Far more discussion is given to the mechanical side of golf than the mental side. A great number of people who are willing to spend a long time perfecting a certain stroke don't bother to think of the many other ways in which they can save strokes on their regular rounds of the course, just by doing a little planning beforehand.

When tournament players go along to play practice rounds before a big tournament they are not just going out to perfect their strokes. They go to survey each hole and take note of the places where shots can easily be wasted. They note such things as out-of-bounds spots; that it is safer to use a three wood instead of a driver from the tee to avoid a ditch; that they must be well up to the pin at the 12th, as all the trouble is on the front of the green and there is none at the back; that there is a deceptive hollow in front of the 18th which makes the shot

The *1968* American Open Champion, Lee Trevino. Lee, one of the great characters of the game, is a real favourite on the practice ground

look much shorter than it really is.

Here is an interesting little story illustrating ho
important it is to think well. I was once playing in
tournament at Little Island, Cork, and I was lying we
up in the second round. I needed to get round in 67
lead the field, which in fact, I managed to do. I wa
playing with Peter Alliss and I took out my driver on th
17th hole. The fairway there sloped quite steeply fro
right to left, with an out-of-bounds area on the left an
bushes on the right.

I hit my drive and faded the ball from left to right an
it finally finished bang in the middle of the fairway.
picked up my tee and walked off the teeing ground an
I saw Alliss come on to the tee with his hands over h
eyes. 'My gosh, you must have some courage or you'r
mad', he exclaimed. 'Why?', I asked. 'Fancy playing
shot like that at a moment like this', he answered. 'But
know I can drive it straight. I could hit the fairway a
day long with that shot', I went on. Anyhow, Peter the
teed up his ball and hit a two iron straight towards th
bushes on the right!

I was simply so confident I would bang it down th
middle that the fact that I needed a good finish for a 6
didn't worry me. Doubts crept into Peter's mind and h
played a poor shot, despite trying to play safe with a
iron.

'It's all in the mind' is a famous saying, and a ver
true one when it comes to golf. In any type of golf th
best way to look at a round is like this. Just concentrat
on your game and on scoring the figures you know yo
are capable of. The golden rule is not to worry abou

20

what your partner is doing, just pay full attention to your own game. If you do that then it is more than likely that your opponent will beat himself.

The hardest man to beat is the quiet one. Don't give any secrets away by saying, 'I only half-hit that one but it got there'. Just smile to yourself if it turns out fine. Your partner or opponent will find it much harder to beat you if he doesn't know what you are thinking.

The whole question of expecting the best in golf is vital. It is completely useless to go out for a round expecting the worst all the time. But that is exactly what many people do. Just stop and think how many times you have heard members at your club before a monthly medal tell their pals that they are going to play badly because they haven't touched a club for three weeks. They may well not have touched a club for three weeks, but if they go out thinking that because of this they are going to top every drive along the ground, the odds are that they will. Go out with the attitude, '*despite* the fact that I haven't touched my clubs for three weeks, I still feel I know and can trust my game enough to drive well'; then straight away your chances of hitting well off the tee will improve.

If you change your mental approach on the course to belief instead of disbelief, you will be amazed by the progress your game makes. One of the world's most famous psychologists, William James, once said: 'Our belief at the beginning of a doubtful undertaking is the one thing that ensures the successful outcome of the venture.' When you expect the best, you release a magnetic force in your mind which, by a law of attraction, tends to bring out the best in you. On the other hand, if you expect the worst, you release from your mind the power of repulsion which tends to force the worst from you.

It is amazing how many golfers, both technically good and technically bad, think wrongly. They stand out there on the tee and expect to hook their drive. Their mental pattern on the golf course is one not of expectation but of doubt. This negative mental process inhibits them, freezes their muscles and harms their timing. But how different things are if the thought pattern is changed; if you begin thinking in terms of expectation instead of doubt when you stand on the tee; if you start to expect the best, not the worst; if you start to think of splitting the fairway with a superb, power-packed drive. If you constantly cram your mind with these sort of thoughts, then the chances are that they will come true.

Things become better when you expect the best instead of the worst for the simple reason that, being freed from self-doubt, you can put your whole self into your endeavour. And nothing can stand in the way of a man who focuses his entire self on one particular problem. When the entire concentration of all your force is brought to bear, the consolidation of these powers properly employed is quite irresistible.

Expecting the best means that you put your whole heart into what you want to accomplish. Too many golfers are defeated on the course not because of lack of ability, but for lack of wholeheartedness. They do not, in other words, wholeheartedly expect to hit a good shot. Their heart isn't in it, which is to say that they themselves are not fully given to the stroke they are about to play.

There are many professional golfers who have gone through their entire career keeping something in reserve. In other words, they do not throw themselves 100 per cent into an event. Because of that fact they have never realised their full potential.

A friend once told me a very good story of how positive thinking can help. The story is in fact based round a trapeze artist, but it can apply equally well to the golfer who stands on the 18th tee needing a birdie to clinch the monthly medal. A trapeze artist of some fame was telling his pupils the best way to perform on the high trapeze bar. After giving a complete rundown on what to do, he instructed the students to have a bash at it themselves.

There was one student, who looked up at the insecure platform from which he was going to perform, and was filled with terror. He just didn't know whether he was coming or going, and conjured up visions of himself falling to the ground. His fright was so intense that he could hardly move a muscle. 'I can't do it, I can't do it', he gasped. The instructor then came up to the poor boy and put his arm round his shoulder and said: 'Boy, you can do it, and I will tell you how.'

Then he said something which has helped me overcome many problems out on the golf course during my tournament career. He said: 'Throw your heart over the bar and your body will follow.' In other words, don't stand on the tee worrying about the rough on the right and the out-of-bounds on the left. Be brave and just aim for the centre of the fairway, however tense the match may be.

It is obvious that you cannot achieve the best in golf, or for that matter, in anything, if you do not know exactly what you want and where you want to go. Too many golfers approach a hole and stand on the tee without setting themselves a target to aim for. In other words, if you are an 18-handicap player, you might set yourself a target of a four at a particularly tough par three hole. It is better to do this than to play the hole with a vague hope that if you are lucky you might just make a par.

Many golfers never get a good round in simply because they do not know or define what they want to do. They have no clear-cut and defined purpose, when they tee off at the first. You cannot expect the best if you think aimlessly. If your golf game seems not to be improving as it should, it is good to remember that you will have to get your ideas organised before you can expect to start getting that handicap down. Set yourself a target each time you play, even if it is only the number of putts you take. Keep a check on your rounds. That way you can see what part of your game really needs improving and you can take steps to put it right.

A good slogan to remember is: 'No objective leads to no end.' Remember that saying next time you play a round. Any psychologist will tell you that the person who thinks with positive self-reliance and optimism magnetises his condition and releases power to attain his goal. In other words, expect to hit good shots; never let it enter your head that you might play bad shots. Avoid entertaining the concept of the worst, for whatever you take into your mind can grow there. Therefore, make a real point of taking the best into your mind.

This principle works almost everywhere. The salesman makes use of it more than most people. The successful salesman approaches the customer expecting to sell his goods. He envisages positive, not negative, results. It is an accepted principle that what the mind profoundly expects it tends to receive. Unless you really want something sufficiently to create an atmosphere of positive factors by your dynamic desire, it is likely to elude you.

To improve your thinking on a golf course is not easy. Nothing that is worthwhile is easy. But just as it is vital to practise your driving if you want to get your swing into a groove, it is equally vital to practise the art of expectation. It is a fact that nobody masters anything except by intensive and intelligent practice. So next time you step out on to the course make a point of thinking better by expecting the best. Results will not come quickly, but by solid practice they will be achieved eventually, and when they are, just watch your handicap come down. The other members will wonder what has come over you as you consistently produce good rounds.

In this connection I always think of a story concerning the great American tennis player, Pancho Gonzales. In his early days he won a championship of some considerable importance. Because of poor weather conditions he had not had very many opportunities to sharpen up his game. One tennis writer, in a summing-up piece on the championship, praised Gonzales for his powerful service and good volley, but said that there were certain defects in his techniques and commented that better champions had displayed their ability on the courts.

The writer concluded that the factor that really won Gonzales this title was his staying power and the further point that 'he was never defeated by the discouraging vicissitudes of the game'. In other words, when things seemed to go against him he did not let any discouragement creep in or let any negative thoughts dominate and, as a result, lose the power needed to gain victory. It was this great mental quality that made Gonzales the champion. And he was able to face obstacles and, indeed, overcome them.

That is a marvellous story and one that every golfer would do well to remember. If you remember this story when things are going badly out on the course then there is every chance that you will persuade yourself to buckle down to the job in hand. It is common knowledge that anybody can keep going when the going is good, when things are going your way, but something extra is required to help you keep fighting hard when it seems everything is going against you.

A book which will help many golfers is *The Power of Positive Thinking* by the famous Norman Vincent Peale. It is a book which has helped Gary Player *(5)* tremendously. In it there is a magnificent story which I think every club golfer would do very well to read. Peale writes:

I played golf with a man who was not only an excellent golfer but a philosopher as well. As we went around the golf course the game itself drew out of him certain gems of wisdom for one of which I shall ever be grateful.

The great little South African, Gary Player, in his familiar black outfit. Gary has benefited, as I have, from reading Norman Vincent Peale's book The Power of Positive Thinking

I hit a ball into the rough, into some high grass. When we came up to my ball, I said in some dismay: 'Now just look at that. I certainly am in the rough. I have a bad lie. It is going to be tough getting out of here.'

My friend grinned and said: 'Didn't I read something about positive thinking in your books?'

Sheepishly I acknowledged that such was the case.

'I wouldn't think negatively about that lie of yours', he said. 'Do you think you could get a good hit if this ball were lying out on the fairway on the short grass?'

I said I thought so.

'Well', he continued, 'why do you think you could do better out there than here?'

'Because', I replied, 'the grass is cut short on the fairway and the ball can get away better.'

Then he did a curious thing. 'Let's get down on our hands and knees', he suggested, 'and examine the situation. Let's see just how this ball does lie.'

So we got down on our hands and knees and he said: 'Observe that the relative height of the ball here is about the same as it would be on the fairway, the only difference being that you have about five or six inches of grass above the ball.'

Then he did an even more whimsical thing. 'Notice the quality and character of this grass', he said. He pulled off a blade and handed it to me. 'Chew it', he said.

I chewed and he asked: 'Isn't that tender?'

'Why, yes', I replied. 'It certainly does seem to be tender grass.'

'Well', he continued, 'an easy swing of your number five iron will cut through that grass almost like a knife.' And then he gave me this sentence which I am going to remember as long as I live, and I hope you will also.

'The rough is only mental.' 'In other words', he

continued, 'it is rough because you think it is. In your mind you have decided that there is an obstacle which will cause you difficulty. The power to overcome this obstacle is in your mind. If you visualise yourself lifting that ball out of the rough, believing you can do it, your mind will transfer flexibility, rhythm, and power to your muscles and you will handle that club in such a manner that the ball will rise right out of there in a beautiful shot. All you need to do is to keep your eye on that ball and tell yourself that you are going to lift it out of that grass with a lovely stroke. Let the stiffness and tension go out of you. Hit it with exhilaration and power. Remember, the rough is only mental.'

To this day I remember the thrill, the sense of power and delight I had in the clean shot that dropped the ball to the edge of the green.

That is a very great fact to remember in connection with difficult problems—'the rough is only mental'.

Well, I guarantee that the next time you hit your drive into the rough your next shot will be a good one if you remember that little story. It has helped me enormously and if you train your mind to think like that then the rough holds no terrors for you.

The philosopher Thoreau once remarked that the secret of achievement is to hold a picture of a successful outcome in the mind. Next time you play a round of golf, just try holding a successful picture of yourself playing in the mind. Picture yourself playing each hole perfectly and you will be pleasantly surprised how quickly your game improves.

A tip I find useful is: when I have a vital drive, or any important shot, I tell myself I am enjoying playing this shot. I am really happy about playing it. When I do this I more often than not hit a good one. So many club golfers address their ball almost dreading the thought of hitting—and probably a mere half a crown depends on the outcome. Next time you have to hit a good drive to clinch a glass of whisky in the 19th, just tell yourself that you are looking forward to striking the ball. Tell yourself you can't wait to get over it and crack it on its way.

Tension is one of the biggest reasons why a golfer hits a bad shot when a good one is most needed. How often club players stand on the tee all tensed up and, after a long, agonising minute, finally take the club back and then probably just trickle the ball off the tee. I am sure you have seen it countless times.

To play good golf there must be a flow of easy power through every stroke and also through the mind itself. The best way to hit a golf ball is by the easy method, where all the muscles are flexible and operating in correct fashion. If you try to do the ball a nasty injury on the tee you will more likely than not make a terrible mess of the whole thing.

All the great players in the history of the game have appeared to make the game simple. They all had rhythm and an uncanny way of making it all look very, very easy. Just look at players on the tee the next time you see golf on television. Notice how relaxed they look and how easy they make the game seem. It is not hard to see that the top golfers appear to do things very easily and with an absolute minimum of effort. In doing this they release maximum power. Look at the American Ryder Cup man, Julius Boros. He looks so relaxed on the course that you think any minute he might fall off to sleep. And yet when he is on the tee he sends the ball as far as most people. You will never hit the ball properly if you take a huge lunge at it. Just relax and picture a nice, easy, free-flowing swing in your mind.

'It's all very well saying relax on the course, but how do I do it?' you will probably be saying. Well, I have a way to do it and if you give it a try before the next important round of golf you play you will be amazed how effective it proves. You can do this little exercise in your car or in a quiet corner in the locker room just before you go out to play.

First of all, just collapse physically. Let go of every muscle in the body and see yourself as something like a jellyfish with your body in a loose state. Next, form a mental picture of a full sack of coal. Then mentally open the bag and allow the coal to tumble out over the floor. Now all the time think of yourself as the bag—after all, there are not many things more relaxed than an empty sack of coal. Now you are relaxed you must drain the mind—get rid of all worried thoughts, forget your apprehension about those four-foot putts, and about that terrible tee shot you have to hit at the sixth across that wicked old lake. Cast out all these thoughts. In other words, keep the mind drained of all things which would impede the flow of relaxed power. Now you should be ready to go out and play a relaxed round of golf.

When you are out on the course and things are going

against you, a useful tip to help relax is to breathe deeply and make sure you keep your temper. If you don't, then anything can happen—and usually does. I practise breathing deeply before every tournament round I play.

I have purposely devoted a good deal of space to the mental side of the game because I firmly believe that it is the key to good golf. If you can develop these positive thoughts and make them a habit, your game will improve by leaps and bounds.

It is also necessary to remember that a man might have the prettiest swing in the world, but if his thinking on the course is wrong, he will never make the grade. I know many players of my own age who have far better swings than I have. These chaps often beat me in practice rounds, but very rarely in the actual tournaments. This is only due to their mental attitude.

Good thinking is what makes a man a champion. All the champions of today have this in common: they are all masters of themselves. In other words, they don't let themselves be beaten by themselves. Start today to develop a more positive attitude on the course, and you won't be beaten by yourself.

2 The grip

There has never been a decent golfer with a bad grip. A bad grip can only produce inconsistency. I do not know any professional who has a grip which can't be said to be sound, except the Scottish Ryder Cup player Eric Brown *(6)*, whose right hand is under the shaft and whose left hand shows more knuckles than we normally teach.

People who have bad grips have their hands fighting each other. The weakest grip is the one-knuckle, left-handed grip with the right hand underneath the shaft. Instead of showing the back of the right hand, you can see fingers. The grip is most definitely one of the foundations of the golf game, the starting point of everything. No player who grips the club poorly can play consistent golf.

Nearly all the top players in the world at the moment use the *Vardon grip*, in which the fingers of one hand overlap or are linked with the fingers of the other hand. This is the grip I personally recommend and it is quite a coincidence because I learnt my golf in the Channel Islands and played on the course where the great Harry Vardon learnt his golf. Vardon went on to win six Open Championships and became one of the legends of golf. If I win just three Opens I won't grumble too much!

This Vardon grip to me is the most comfortable,

although I have tried the *interlocking* and *double-handed grips*. With the latter I could hit a long ball but couldn't produce any consistency, and the former hurt my fingers. I use a one-knuckle, left-handed grip because I have always been prone to hooking the ball. Since playing in tournaments I have realised that a flat hook is the worst possible shot a professional can hit, because it runs off line as well as twisting off line through the air.

When I won the RTV tournament in 1968 I felt that my left thumb was completely on the top of the shaft, giving me a one-knuckle grip. This meant I could hit as hard as I wanted to with the right hand and still not hook the ball. This was a wonderful feeling to achieve and gave me added confidence, especially when the pressure was on.

The Vardon grip prevents the hands separating during the swing and means both hands work together; but the adjustment of the ten fingers is capable of so many small variations that very few amateur players hold the club correctly.

All beginners feel uncomfortable when they first try the Vardon grip and this is a very good reason why there are so many substitutes for it. With considerable practice, the first uneasiness soon goes, the grip becomes automatic and the role of the right and left hands is co-ordinated. From the beginning, however, the sensible golfer learns to examine his hands to ensure his grip is correct when things go wrong.

Most top tournament players switch from the Vardon grip when they putt, generally using the reverse overlap grip with all the fingers of the right hand on the shaft of

Scottish Ryder Cup player, Eric Brown, whose grip is unusual. His right hand is under the shaft and the left hand shows more knuckles than we normally teach

the putter.

The grip largely decides the position of the club-face as it strikes the ball. A strong swing is impossible without

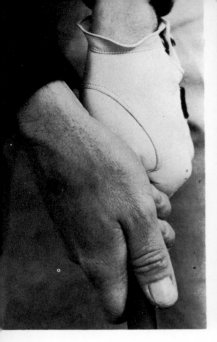

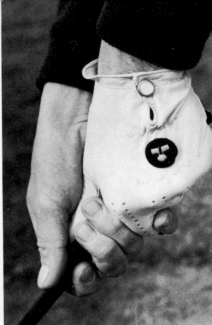

Overlapping grip. Thumb and forefinger of the right hand form a 'v' which should point to the right shoulder. Two and a half knuckles of the left hand is recommended, left thumb on top of the shaft

8 *Side view of the recommended overlapping grip. Note the three fingers of the right hand gripping the shaft, little finger of the right hand resting on the index finger of the left hand*

the correct grip. This does not mean that all good golfers grip the club the same way, for the obvious reason that the shape and strength of people's hands vary a fair amount.

The basic link between you and your golf club has to suit you and nobody else, and when you begin it pays to spend considerable time studying the parts that make up a correct grip. I recommend to pupils that once they get a good grip they must not alter it. Alter the position of the ball in relation to the body—but don't change your grip. This is very important.

When you begin, never feel inhibited. Picture the shot in your mind and carry it out with confidence. Accuracy and length are the two standards by which all shots are judged—and both these attributes depend initially on the grip, and comfort. The basic principles of the Vardon grip also apply to all others.

The Vardon grip
To hold the club, let the shaft sit in the left hand, where the fingers join the palm. Fold the left hand around the shaft with the left thumb a little to the right of the top centre of the club. The other three fingers are closed on the grip and pressure is applied between these fingers and the pad of the hand.

The index finger and thumb of the right hand provide the touch or feel on the club, and the leverage. The other three fingers wrap the shaft against the palm so that it cannot turn, but they are not held so tightly that they become stiff. The left-hand pressure fingers are the fourth finger and little finger. These prevent the club wavering at the top of the swing.

The back of the left hand should point where you aim to hit the ball, and the v formed by the forefinger and the thumb should point between the chin and the right shoulder *(7)*. The left hand guides the club and keeps the club-face in position so that it strikes the ball correctly on impact. The left wrist must be firm at impact and

37

must never collapse.

You will notice that most professionals, including myself, wear a glove on their left hand. If you tend to sweat a little the light, close-fitting gloves made these days prevent the club slipping. The material wrapped around the top of club shafts today has done much to prevent the hands slipping. Leather adheres to leather far better than bare skin to leather or rubber grips.

After gripping the club correctly in the left hand, place the little finger of the right hand over the index or forefinger of the left hand, curling it around the exposed knuckle of the left index finger *(8)*. Then fold the right hand around the grip so that the index finger of the left hand sits against the third finger of the right hand. The thumb of the right hand should be positioned slightly to the left of the centre of the shaft.

The middle fingers of the right hand do the work by putting on pressure strong enough to stop the club slipping but not so tight that the grip feels strained. The thumb and index finger of this hand steady the co-ordinated grip and keep the player in touch with his club by giving that essential feel and leverage.

The complete grip has to be firm enough to withstand a high-speed swing, the curling action of the wrists on the backswing, and the effect of striking the ball, without loosening its power over the club. The grip has to remain the same throughout the swing, without slipping.

Sores sometimes form on the pressure fingers of both hands. These are only caused by letting go or a bad grip. If the grip is correct, the hands should not feel sore even after two rounds on the same day.

9　British Ryder Cup man Dai Rees—he has used the baseball grip
with great success

10   The big, powerful American
Jack Nicklaus, sends another golf b
its way. Jack has used the interlockin

The two most popular grips after the Vardon are the
baseball or *double-handed grip* and the *interlocking grip.*

Baseball and interlocking grips
With the baseball grip, the hands do not overlap and all
ten fingers are placed on the shaft. British Ryder Cup
man Dai Rees *(9)* has used this grip to great success.
Rees can use this grip because he is not a big man and he

has smallish hands. The grip enables him to get more leverage; I recommend all golfers with small hands to use it.

The interlocking grip has been employed by the great American, Jack Nicklaus *(10)*. In the interlocking grip the hands are linked by thrusting the little finger of the right hand between the index and second finger of the left hand.

The grip which you decide is right for you must remain constant throughout the swing. Many golfers go wrong in altering their grip on the surprisingly severe impact with the ball. It really is vital to sustain a compact, unchanged grip throughout the swing. You can adjust the tightness of the grip when you first address the ball, holding the club-shaft with relaxed firmness. Retain this pressure throughout the swing and remember that the action of the swing is so fast that application of more power through slight variations of the grip is impossible.

Basically, the principle to follow is: hold the club right when you address the ball and never alter that grip. Ask your local professional if your grip is correct and have confidence in it.

I have studied people when they are playing under pressure and they seem to squeeze their hands together far too much. You can even see the veins in their hands, which is a bad thing, because if you get tension in your muscles you can't use them properly. Under pressure relax your grip a little. This will relax your arms and you will play a lot better.

Tension is a common fault among nearly all golfers,

from the man trying to win the Open to the club golfer striving to clinch his victory in a medal. It is the cause of most of their bad shots near the end of the round when good shots are usually most needed.

3   The stance

Most professionals adopt a fairly wide stance with the driver, with the right foot slightly behind the left, in other words the right foot drawn back an inch or two from the intended line of flight. This wide stance enables the club to go back to a full arc.

It really is amazing how careless many golfers are about the way they position their feet in relation to the ball; this carelessness is the cause of poor aiming and failure to use clubs well. The golfer very often won't even place his club-face behind the ball, make sure it is squarely across the direction line, then arrange his feet, body and hands in proper relation to the ball.

Many people fail to realise that clubs are designed to be used with a correct stance. The clubmaker designs and manufactures clubs to be used with a swing that is basically the same for every shot, except for the power required. That is why the type of shot is determined to a great extent by where the arc of the swing brings the 'sweet spot' of the club-face into precise contact with the ball.

With a long iron, the basic position for the ball with a normal lie is halfway between the inner edges of the heels, the heels about as far apart as the shoulder tips, the hands to be just about in the same plane as the ball. With the club flat on the ground and the middle of the club-face squarely back of the ball, angle and length of the club decide the distance of the feet from the imaginary direction line that runs through the ball. The arms should hang down easily so the hands are fairly close to the body.

The posture is fairly erect, with the knees loose and bent just a little. The main departure from vertical is at the neck. There's no stooping, stretching or squatting in the posture that permits a free body turn and retains stability.

This basic stance is square, that is, with toes on a line parallel with the direction line, and turned out slightly as one normally stands. This square stance with the ball in the middle position is the stance for the fairway woods and the five iron and irons of lesser loft. The stance recommended for the drive has the ball slightly inside the left heel. The hands are a bit behind the plane of the club-face *(11)*.

Many club golfers have the ball teed in a line off the left toe, or even a bit further to the left. Then it is physically impossible to drive without falling into the ball. When you lunge into the ball almost anything but a good shot can result. Then the player tells himself that he teed the ball too high and hit under it. But what really happened was that the club turned as he fell into the ball and he hit with the forward part of the top of the club.

The right foot should be turned slightly to the right when you're playing with a closed stance. That little bit of pointing outward by your right foot will ease the strain on your right thigh—and probably on your back, because you have to twist around a lot as well as using a perfectly-timed hand action to generate power for your

44

*Note the position of the ball in rela-
tion to the left foot from the front view,
feet shoulder-width apart*

drive. Unless your feet are in position to reduce strain
on your back muscles and your spine, you are always
prone to an annoying injury. Young players who are
strong and flexible can get away with considerable strain
on the back for a while, but eventually it catches up even

45

12   Driving : both arms extended, comfortable start

with them.

Personally, I like to use a fairly open stance *(12)* because when I first started, as I wrote in Chapter 2, I used to hook the ball, and this was partly because I had a shut stance. The shut stance stopped my body from

46

following through. If you get your left foot in the way too much the left side is blocked and it is impossible for your body to follow through. Consequently, with my four-knuckle grip, I used to use my hands a lot and my body only a little. This fault was what produced my hook and must be avoided at all costs.

People who use a conventional two-knuckle grip should have their left foot back just slightly to allow their body to follow through. Then they can hit hard with their hands and not have the body in the way. In other words, you get a better coordination with your body and hands from a slightly open stance.

It is a great fault to think that a shut stance will help gain distance. This is not so, as it blocks the hit and can produce either a flat hook or a cut, depending on the hand action and position of the club-face.

I believe a golfer's movements should have complete freedom, and this open stance gives freedom which is very necessary for a big drive. Middle-aged or older golfers will find it much easier to swing if the feet are placed a little closer together than normal.

You will have to experiment in finding out the correct distance between your feet for the various strokes. I usually recommend to pupils that the longer the shot, the wider apart the feet should be, within reasonable bounds. When the feet are too far apart, you might well lock your body on the backswing and sway instead of turn. On the long irons your feet should be closer than they are for the woods. Your feet get closer together as the club loft increases.

Being a small man, people often ask me if I have any

special tips for small golfers. On the whole a small man ought to adopt a narrow stance and a tall man a wide stance. The tall man, of course, has already the advantage of a wide arc, so getting his feet further apart to get good balance can only help him. If the small man had a wide stance he would restrict his movement, and he wouldn't use his hands so much. A person will use his hands and arms more if he has a narrow stance. This allows his body complete freedom of movement.

When I want to hit a long shot I get my feet close together so that my body can turn and this in turn lengthens my swing; obviously if you use a long swing you hit the ball further than if you use a short swing.

Remember though, a long shot does not allow a fast backswing. It is important to swing back slower in an effort to reach the correct position at the top of the swing. Then you can swing faster—*on the way back to the ball!*

4   The swing

The hands should start the backswing by drawing the club away along the ground and slightly inside the line of flight. The club continues in as wide an arc as possible

*Club-head starting
k, on the inside
ve in a wide arc*

14 *Wide sweep with club-head, shoulders and hips turning*

(13) behind the player rather than above him and if the
left arm is extended the club should arrive halfway back
with the face of the club still pointing to the ball—in other
words, facing square throughout the swing if possible.

The worst fault is to roll the face open. It's been
proved by scientists in the book, *The Search for the*

Perfect Swing, which was prepared and written for the Golf Society of Great Britain, that open-face players, the ones who roll the club-face open and then closed, are the most inconsistent. If the club-face can be held square to the ball throughout the swing, this will produce consistency and a good trajectory.

15   Full pivot, wrists fully curled, left knee relaxed

16 Correct wris
arm position at th
of the swing. Wris
arm in a straight
right elbow down

17 Incorrect wrist
position at the top of
the swing. Left wrist
has dropped, causing
face to be too shut

52

On the way back the weight must shift from 50 per cent on either foot to roughly 75 per cent on the right foot at the top of the backswing. To get the weight on to the right foot, turn the shoulders and the hips so that at the top of the swing the shoulders are at an angle of 90 degrees to the line of flight, and the hips approximately 45 degrees *(14, 15)*.

At the top of the swing the right elbow should have buckled, so that it points towards the ground and not behind or into the air. The right elbow must be underneath the left arm, and pointing to the ground.

The left arm naturally should be kept straight and the left wrist firm, not cupped or twisted as people with very open-face swings do *(16, 17)*. Remember, keep the left arm straight but not rigid. If the club-face is held square to the line throughout the swing, the left wrist will be in a straight line at the top of the swing.

The left thumb should be supporting the shaft at the top of the swing. If you cup your wrists or turn your left wrist backwards, this will mean that the left arm is not supporting the shaft and the club will slip.

The right hand at the top of the swing should be like a waiter's hand when he carries a tray over his shoulder. The palm of the hand should be parallel to the sky, and the right arm should be facing the ground in the horizontal position so that the right wrist is bent back fully.

The club at this position should be parallel to the ground with the club-face almost turned towards the sky—in other words, not completely shut but very square. This will produce a fully wound-up position which gives power and accuracy.

18 *Top of swing : correct position, front view*

19 *Top of swing : incorrect position, view—too much weight on left foot*

At this point the left heel should be raised only an inch or so off the ground, not two or three inches as many handicap players do. The left leg must not buckle at the knee. It is vital to be correctly balanced at the top of the swing *(18–21)*.

Quite a number of beginners ask me about the Doug Sanders swing—the short, punchy affair which has earned colourful Doug so many dollars on the rich American circuit. I would not recommend this swing to the average club golfer. Doug has been playing this way

Top of swing, front view : incorrect—
~uch weight on right foot

21 *Top of swing, front view : incorrect—*
swing too upright, no shoulder or hip turn,
stiff-legged

for a long time and is very strong, but most club golfers have not got strong hands and can't accelerate the club enough from the position which Sanders gets in. It's true that the shorter the swing, the less chance there is of errors creeping in, but I believe most club golfers would rather sacrifice a little accuracy to get distance, and it's very hard to get distance from a short swing.

Undoubtedly the most satisfying shot in golf is a long straight drive. For women in particular it is physically a little more difficult to swing the club far back, but I still

55

22　*The late hit : correct position*

23　*The late hit : incorrect position–
too late, this should be avoided at all*

recommend a long swing rather than a shorter swing.
Women just cannot hit the ball far enough with a short
swing. They must use their body and their hips to get a
fully wound-up position. This is the only way in which
they can really hit the ball a long way. I have noticed
that most women, and many men too, have weak wrists.
If they exercise their wrists they could manage the
shorter swing, but since most amateur golfers are not
prepared to do all the exercises that are recommended,
the only way they can get length is to make up for it
with a big backswing, and plenty of movement. It's like

56

Correct head position—head slightly
d the ball

25 Incorrect head position—head too far
behind the ball, front view at impact

a spring. If you don't wind it up properly it won't unwind.

In the past, British teachers have taught wrists and arms for club-head acceleration. This isn't the complete answer. A big wind-up and a wide arc will produce more speed than a quick, narrow swish with the wrists.

The first movement of the downswing is to return the left heel to the ground. This will get the weight over to the left foot and into the hitting position, and you will find that just moving the left heel down will also bring the arms down halfway, and contribute to a good, late

26 *Incorrect head position—head too far in front of ball*

27 *Hips unwinding, right knee kicking in, hands and arms accelerating club-head*

28 *Well-balanced, firm hitting position*

hitting action. Remember to get into the correct hitting position before accelerating the club towards the ball (22–26).

It's from this position that you start accelerating the club with your hands and arms. You have now got your weight behind the ball and now you have to use your arms and your hands to accelerate the club as fast as you like, providing the club keeps on a straight line (27, 28).

Don't hit across your body, always hit out towards the target. In other words, keep the club on the line of flight as long as possible.

At impact, the club must be held firmly and both arms must be extended (29). If, as happens to many players, the left arm and wrist collapse, the club will swing across the ball and across one's body and this will produce crooked shots.

29 *Impact : firm left side, steady head position*

30 *Well-balanced follow-through, club-head continuing to good finish*

The left arm must be braced; the right hand supplies most of the power and must extend after hitting the ball so that two feet after impact both arms are completely straight and the club-head should be travelling at its fastest at this position.

If the left foot is not raised too much on the backswing, then it is fine just to stamp your left heel down, but if the left foot has risen two or three inches it must be lowered carefully in order to make sure that the heel is brought down in the correct position. If the left foot doesn't move very far in the backswing it doesn't have to move very far in the downswing. At impact both feet should be flat on the ground with the right knee turning in towards the left to help the balance and create speed.

The follow-through now is very important *(30)*. I often notice that very few amateurs follow through correctly. And I can easily see that the most common faults are that the left arm and wrist buckles, the left foot moves incorrectly, and the whole left side of the body is useless—it puts up no resistance and therefore the club-head travels across the body and across the line of flight, producing either a terrible slice (if the wrists aren't used properly) or a duck hook if the club comes down square.

The left side *must* be braced, the left arm *must* be braced and the power is supplied with the right hand and right side. Both arms must extend through towards the hole.

A good way to practise the follow-through is to swing a club with your left hand, trying to keep the left arm straight, but not rigid, throughout the swing. Nearly everyone to whom I have recommended this has reported excellent results. If the arm can be kept straight this will produce a high finish like Arnold Palmer's. They call it the picture-frame finish. An excellent exercise this—you can even do it in the garden at home.

Any exercise with the hands and arms is good. When I was younger I read Henry Cotton's books on this subject of strengthening the hands and I used to practise with a heavy club trying to hit the ball out of rough. If you can hit a good shot with a heavy club from quite thick rough then your hands are strong enough to take the strain at impact. Even now I swing heavy clubs and practise shots from rough to keep fit and strong.

I don't believe that the basic golf method will change very much in the years to come. Vardon and Jones had swings which still work and are considered classical even today. The methods haven't changed very much over the years. They just haven't always been explained properly, in my opinion.

Recently people have gone into great detail using science and muscle control. This to me is unnecessary. The amateur golfer looks at this information and often throws it away immediately because he cannot understand it. Some try these things out and end up with their local pro, needing to be put back on their game. Tuition must be simplified if people are going to play well.

The only time you should get technical about the game is when you are a really good player and some small thing goes wrong and you can't discover the fault and have to start all over again. This frequently happens with

61

tournament players. The best example is Scotland's Eric Brown who went to America three or four years ago only to find that his long game went off completely. Eric had won many tournaments and yet suddenly it all left him. He had to leave the States and come straight back and start all over again to build it up. Now, although he is not a young man, he is still winning money in tournaments.

It's the simple method which is best. Harry Vardon's method was probably the simplest ever and he won six Open Championships. The Great Triumvirate, Vardon, Taylor, and Braid, stayed good for a long time because they had simple methods, particularly Vardon. There were no fancy bits about his swing. Dai Rees and Max Faulkner are lasting a long time for a similar reason—their basic methods are sound. They don't have flying right elbows or twisting wrist actions. After you get a good method it's up to your temperament to decide how good you are going to be.

Every golfer must have some style. I know one or two people who are very stout and they take the club straight back, at least halfway back, and then push it straight through. They cannot hit the ball very far, but they keep it in play all the time. And their method is as sound as anyone's. There is not much of it, but what there is is correct.

A good swing and good temperament can go a very long way. Confidence in one's method is essential to a reasonable player. The British players, I believe, are as good as players from any other country in the world, when it comes to accuracy with the long game.

I base all my knowledge in my writing on the experience of travelling and playing golf in different countries. I have played this game in Europe, South Africa, the Far East, America, and Canada, and I have always been very interested in the golf swing, because when I first started I realised I was small and I had to find a method which would help me compete with the 15-stone men. I was not very strong and very slim. It was, I feel, because of this that I held the club with a four-knuckle, left-hand grip and used an extremely long backswing. I could even see the club out of the corner of my eye at the top of the swing.

I continued doing this for some years, until my late teens, when I became an assistant in Jersey. C. T. Tudor, my employer in those days, was always telling me that my swing was a bit too long, but he wanted me to be as natural as possible. So he made me practise as much as possible. For this I am extremely grateful. I was able to work things out by myself with the occasional correction from him. He didn't believe in changing me too much because I was a fairly good player at that time. But when I moved on to Ham Manor in Sussex, W. T. Twine, the professional at the club, insisted that I shortened the swing because I was getting into trouble with long, looping hooks.

I took the advice and did shorten my swing. I worked very hard at this for two years, strengthening my hands and getting my left hand into a better position. Twine was a great advocate of the one-knuckle grip. He used this grip very successfully in tournaments in the days of Henry Cotton.

The change to a shorter swing began to pay dividend for me after about two years and I won the odd local event, which gave me great encouragement. I then decided to try my luck on the major circuit. In my second year on the circuit something happened which had a profound effect on the rest of my golfing career: I met Max Faulkner.

Max has become a great friend of mine and I consider he has helped me in tournament golf more than anyone else I know. He never stops encouraging me and I owe him much of my success. It was Max who got me back to a more normal position at the top of the swing with the club parallel to the ground.

So there it is, quite a story behind my swing. I went from a very long swing to an extremely short one which enabled me to hit the ball fairly straight, but as time went on I realised that if I was going to play with, and beat, the big hitters, such as Nicklaus and Thomas, had to do something to increase my distance and reverted, with Max Faulkner's help, to a more normal swing.

Most experts will agree when they see the photographs in this book that my position at the top of the swing is fairly standard. It is firm, I hold the club in the normal manner, and I am able to hit the ball hard with my hands with this swing. Naturally, since I have lengthened my swing, I have gained much distance and, what is very important, I haven't sacrificed any accuracy.

This is the swing I am going to stick to for the rest of my golfing life. I have gone the whole circle now. From long to short and then back to fairly long again. Now it is fairly normal I don't even worry about it. I am confident that it will work.

5 The drive

The best driver I know is the Ryder Cup player, David Thomas *(31)*. This is because of his wonderful club-head control. The face of his club always points in the direction of his target. The club-face is kept square throughout the scoring. This is technically the most reliable way of swinging the golf club and this is why David is such a good driver.

The drive, as our American friends look at it, is a formality. They just tee the ball up very high and hit it hard with as big a swing as they can possibly get at it. This doesn't mean you should let the club dip down your back, as many women golfers do. They only do this because their hands and arms are weak.

The Americans are the longest drivers in the world, although I would say they are probably not the most accurate. However, distance is the most important part of driving because nowadays we are getting watered fairways and the ball will stop where it lands. Also, tees on all courses are being pushed further and further back, which puts far more emphasis on the long drive than ever before in the history of golf.

I have quite often been asked what you should think about when you stand on the tee. Before you hit the ball, think of where you are going to hit it, and how far you are going to hit, then think of nothing else except swing-

31 Big Dave Thomas, the Welsh Ryder Cup man. Dave's wonderful club-head control makes him the best driver of a golf ball I know

ing the club. Always have confidence in your swing.
Once you start the swing, keep up the rhythm; keep

the rhythm in your mind. Some people have even done it by humming a tune to themselves. Rhythm in this game is the smooth flow of developing details of the swing. It coordinates every element, so there is no jerkiness or neglect of any part of the performance but sound progress to the completion of the job in hand. The rhythm varies in pace being, generally, comparatively slow in the backswing, coming almost to a pause at the top of the backswing, then accelerating in the downswing until the hit is the emphatically accented stage of movement. The follow-through is an echo of the effective rhythm.

It is rhythm that makes a golf swing an expression of a true artist. There are some excellent golfers whose swings are smooth, and every detail is perfectly synchronised, yet their swings have a mechanical look. Those swings are hard work and are suitable only for the few golfers who can devote a tremendous amount of time to them.

Rhythm basically comes from perfect muscular control. It is impossible to achieve rhythm if the body is tense. Muscular control may be instinctive or deliberate or both during a golf swing, and it is this control that enables you to hit the ball. Our muscles instinctively are trying to whack the club-head against the ball, but often we seem to have a tremendous determination to interfere with the impulse. Consequently we are inclined to fight ourselves and rush to hit the ball before we are really ready. Waiting until one is really ready is the really important point to good timing; that all-important pause at the top of the backswing is what allows you to finish the backswing. The club golfer hardly ever completes his backswing before he starts down with a jerk, throwing himself out of balance and aim.

The pause at the top really is the key to effective timing. It is the essential syncopation of the rhythm of a good swing. You've got to have it, it is insurance against throwing away power at the top of the swing where you can't use power. This pause is one of the differences between the swings of the experts and the efforts of poor players.

I myself rarely try to hit the ball at full throttle and rarely take part in long-driving competitions. At the Bowmaker Tourney in 1967, however, I decided to have a go at long driving as I had been hitting the ball extremely well with my driver throughout the Tournament. As I stood on the tee I could feel the tension build up as I got a little excited. After five or six hits I gave up because I had completely lost my rhythm in an effort to gain distance. A couple of days later in the Open at Carnoustie I was one of the few who could find those elusively narrow fairways. I played with Arnold Palmer, who had an unhappy week. Three or four of his drives in each round found the extremely long rough and cost him a high finishing position.

I firmly believe that a golfer should not struggle too much for length if he is not naturally capable of hitting a long ball. It is far more important to concentrate, instead, on a compact swing and use what distance you have.

I missed qualifying for the final two rounds of the 1968 US Masters at Augusta because of foolishly trying to find more distance from the tee as I had been told that golf in America was only for the long hitters. In the first round I started driving into the pine trees that lined the fairways and ruined my chances of scoring decently because of this quest for length. I eventually wound up with a 78. In the second outing I kept the ball on the fairways, forgetting about length, worked like a Trojan on and around the greens and handed in a respectable 73. Unfortunately, I couldn't make up for the shots I wasted in the first round, but in the end I only missed the cut by three strokes.

The moral of all this is that it is absolutely useless doing something which is foreign to you on the course. Under pressure it will break down—in the practice rounds at Augusta I seemed to be hitting the ball long distances and getting away with things, but when the pressure was on my timing went completely.

The really essential thing with driving is to hit the ball straight. If the average assistant professional could hit really straight he would go round courses in 70 or less every time. Instead, what usually happens is that he hits the ball in the middle of the club fairly often, but just cannot hit it consistently straight. If you hit the drive straight and a reasonable distance, then half the battle is won.

Laying down the law about the length or weight of the driver to use, without fitting it to individual needs, would be totally wrong. The old instructional theory used to be that a short man should use a short club and a tall man should use a long one. But students of the game have come to realise that the reverse is nearer to being correct. Manufacturers, however, have standardised the length and weight of golf clubs. The standard length of the driver is 43 inches. Thirteen and a half to 14 ounces is a good weight for the average player's woods.

In selecting your driver, it would be stupid to select a club with considerable whip if you have a short, fast backswing, because you would have difficulty controlling it. If you are older and have a full, slow swing you should use a club with enough flex in the shaft for you to be able to feel the club-head. The weight of the club-head should also be in relation to the flex of the shaft. If you have a stiff, heavy shaft, your club has to have more weight in the club-head so you can get the 'feel' of the club-head during the swing. The lighter and more flexible the shaft, the less weight is needed in the club-head.

In selecting and using wood clubs, it is useful to remember that sometimes a player can change club-heads without getting into trouble, but usually he is asking for problems when he changes the shafts. The reason for this is that the flex and the weight of all shafts are different, and they have a direct effect on the golf swing. If there is any difference in the flex of the shaft from what you are accustomed to, no matter how slight it is, it can throw your swing off.

Give considerable thought to the relationship of the flex of the shaft to your swing before you select your wood clubs. It will be worth your while. But as a general rule, I recommend that a light driver should be used, because it has been proved only recently that, for most golfers, a light club will send the ball further than a heavy club. Speed, not weight, is the important thing.

Two important things for the club golfer to do when he gets on the first tee
1. Have a long, slow practice swing. Anyone who has seen Max Faulkner swing will know what I mean. Before Max hits the ball he has a perfect practice swing in slow motion. He takes the club back as low to the ground as possible, in as wide an arc as possible, has a complete turn of his shoulders, hips, legs, and arms, until he reaches the top of the swing. Then he holds it, checks that it is all right, starts the downswing, and goes through the motions of a perfect swing and follow-through.

Most people pick up a club, have a quick swish and think they are ready to hit the ball, when in fact they are not. In having that quick swish they are likely to have a short backswing, and a follow-through which is far too quick and jerky; this can only produce inconsistency. If they do the whole thing slowly they will probably do a good, slow swing when they hit the ball.

2. If it is a fine day and you are having this slow practice swing turn your back to the sun just to see if your head is moving. Look at the shadow of your head; if this moves while you are swinging, then you are swinging the club incorrectly. The head must not move more than an inch on the backswing or the downswing.

One final point about the drive. Many beginners find it hard to get to a golf club or practice ground every day. This is understandable, and yet you can still keep your eye in by swinging an old heavy club, weighing 18 or

20 ounces, in the garden.

Have a couple of swings each day with this club before going to work, and the improvement in your game will be startling.

6 Fairway woods

The most important thing to remember with fairway-wood shots *(32–41)* is to try to keep the club-head low to the ground for as long as you can. If possible, try and keep the club-head just above the grass for at least a foot going back and at least a foot going through. If this is done, then you get maximum loft from your fairway wood and maximum distance, because if the arc is wide you are able to generate a lot of speed. Also, if you can keep the club-head low to the ground this produces accuracy. Imagine that your club is travelling along the grass for as long as possible. This is the secret of good wood-club play.

The British Ryder Cup man Neil Coles is probably the best fairway-wood player I know. He swings very wide; he uses his weight well; the club goes neither inside nor outside the line of flight, but in a straight line, and stays very low to the ground.

This pattern should also be followed on downhill and uphill lies with the wooden club. Always follow the slope of the ground; use the ground as your guide.

For uphill lies *(42, 43)*, the ball is naturally going to rise, so it is wise to have the ball nearer your right foot— in other words, play the ball in the centre of your feet. The important thing to do with an uphill lie is to keep the ball down, and the way to do this is to keep the

Fairway-wood shot: the address position

33 Note the very square take-away; the club-face has not turned away from the ball

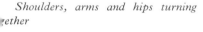

Shoulders, arms and hips turning together

35 Left knee turned in, right leg braced, full shoulder and hip turn, left arm straight but not rigid

36 Weight shifting forward, right knee kicking in, fairly late hit

37 Right knee, arms and hands driv forward

38 Right elbow tucked well in, left side firm

39 Right arm beginning to straight club-head following through low to ground

weight on the left foot and the hands slightly forward. Never try and scoop the shot or hurry it. Just use the same rhythm as with any other shot.

Arms and hands complete the ac-
eration, club-head still facing the target

41   *Poised, well-balanced finish*

42 Uphill lie: correct position, front view—weight slightly on left foot, head over the ball

All this, of course, works in reverse for the downhill stroke *(44, 45)*. Here, obviously, the ball must not rise very high. In order to ensure this, you must have the ball opposite your left foot. Have the hands slightly behind the ball and keep the weight slightly on the right foot. This will mean that the club is travelling low to the ground and is coming down underneath the ball into

43 Uphill lie: incorrect position, front view—too much weight on right foot, head too far behind ball, ball position too far forward

44 *Downhill lie : correct position, front view—weight slightly on left foot, ball positioned well forward*

45 *Downhill lie : incorrect stance—teed too far off right foot*

46 *Christy O'Connor, the popular Irish star, hits a wood from the rough.*
This is one of Christy's favourite strokes, and he plays it to great effect

he air; so, again, don't try and scoop it up.

One of the most frequent questions I am asked by pupils is when one should hit an iron in preference to a wood from the fairway. The answer is this: if there is a long way to go and you have a poorish lie, *still* use a wooden club. The loft on the club will get the ball into the air. It's not necessary to use a chopping blow on the fairway, unless the ball is in an exceptionally bad lie— in this case a five wood is the club to use. Remember to have the ball nearer your right foot so that you hit the ball before the divot.

The only time you should use an iron on the fairway is when the distance is not far enough for a wood. You will get more distance from a five wood than you would from a four iron—a five wood is equal to about a three iron.

Woods from rough

If it is at all possible to get the ball out of the rough with a wood, do so. Use a four wood or five wood, whichever is your favourite. But don't use a low swing in the rough. You just won't get any speed from it because the grass will tangle round the club and slow it down.

An iron club will not get the ball far enough from rough unless it has got a lot of loft and you are very strong. It is much wiser to take a wood providing, naturally, that the rough isn't too long. The average player should use more wood from the fairway, because he cannot hit the ball far enough with an iron.

Club golfers see Irish star, Christy O'Connor *(46)*, playing his fantastic shots from the rough with his four wood and say, 'Oh, I wish I could do that'. But they could if they had a four or five wood because it doesn't require a very different action unless the grass is very long. If one can hit a five iron from the rough then one can hit a five wood from the rough and get further.

People who watch Christy marvel at his shots from the rough, but the reason for his success is that he is a good wooden-club player and this is his favourite shot. He has confidence in his action.

So wherever possible, use your wood. Get that distance which everyone yearns for. Always play the shot with confidence and expect to hit a good one.

Bending the ball from fairways

Now a tip for the more advanced player who wants to hook or slice his ball round a hazard. It's a well-known fact that you can alter your stance to make the ball slice or hook, but in my opinion this is not enough. I think that to slice the ball one should also alter one's grip just slightly. Most people know that a one-knuckle grip will produce a slice and a four-knuckle grip will produce a hook.

When I was a teenager I was told that it was only necessary to alter one's stance. This is only true if you have a first-class swing and, honestly, very few amateurs have that. I myself prefer to make sure of getting enough bend on the ball by moving my left hand—to the left for the slice and to the right for the hook. Your hands control the club-head.

This, of course, is the simplest cure for a hook and a slice. Simply move your left hand. As the left hand guides the club and the right hand supplies the power, use your guiding hand to help you.

Some really good players use a different method: they simply 'feel' the shot by rolling their wrists at impact for the hook and blocking their follow-through by stiffening the left wrist at impact for the cut shot. Thus, the left hand leads for the slice and the right hand works over-time for the hook. This method takes much practice, and is not recommended for the average golfer.

I hope one year to play part of the American Tour, and I will not worry too much about long hitting. I hit the ball just as far as Billy Casper, just as far as Gary Player, and look how well they have done! I have played with both Billy and Gary and they really aren't long hitters, but they are very clever. If you do lack length then obviously you must concentrate on the short game to make up for it, and this will be the way I will approach golf in America.

In America you often need to play wood for your second shot. Gary Player is a great three or four wood player and that is why he has done so well on the other side of the Atlantic. Both he and Billy Casper are able to put the ball as near the pin with a three wood as they can with a four iron. This is a great thing, as the courses in America are often longer than those in Britain. If one lacks a few yards in length then it is essential to hit the ball straight, and if one has to use a three wood rather than a three iron then one has to become a three-wood expert as both Gary and Billy have.

Long and medium irons

Long irons

The British are as good at long-iron shots as any, because we are used to playing into the wind. More British players use a two or one iron than anyone else in the world because of our blustery conditions. Many of the big tournaments are played on seaside courses, which are exposed to the wind, and British players instead of using four or five woods take a one iron or two iron and keep the ball low. The Scottish Ryder Cup player, George Will, is a particularly good long-iron man, and so is Peter Alliss *(47)*. Another excellent long-iron player is the American star Arnold Palmer *(48)*.

The long-iron shot is my favourite stroke. I get more pleasure from hitting a good low two iron into the wind than I do from any other shot in the game. I have made myself a lot of money with this kind of shot, particularly on seaside courses. It is because of that that I always enter the Open Championship, which is always played on seaside links, thinking that I have a good chance of pulling off the big one.

The secret of long-iron play is to keep the ball low and to keep the left wrist firm. One must never let one's left wrist collapse. The long iron and the fairway wood are very similar. The main difference is that you do take a slight divot with the long iron. The ball is played further

47 *Peter Alliss—a good long-iron and hero of several British Ryder teams*

back—the longer the shot, the nearer the left foot the ball is; the shorter the shot, the nearer the right foot it s—and the swing is just a fraction shorter but still firm. You must never be loose at the top of the swing. Most important of all is the straight left wrist at impact and after impact. This is so important because if you collapse with the long iron you get no loft or direction. A very

The legendary American player, ld Palmer. Arnold is a strong long- player

49 A three-iron shot : orthodox grip and stance with feet shoulder-width apart

50 Fairly wide take-away, wrists n● yet starting to curl

51 Shoulders and hips turning together, wrists starting to curl

52 Maximum hip and shoulder tur● wrists fully curled, three-quarter swing ● recommended for medium-iron shot

53 Weight has started to shift to the left foot, delaying the hit

55 Head absolutely still, good balance

54 Weight has now completely shifted the left side, wrists and hands starting accelerate the club-head

56 Good hitting position, right kn moving forwards, hands and arms drivi past the ball

57 *Right knee well forward, head absolutely still, hands continuing to accelerate club-head, left side firm*

58 *A balanced finish of swing, straight left side. N the feet action*

firm grip is needed because a long iron has a small head and so accuracy plays a big part *(49–58)*.

Medium irons

The best medium-iron player I have seen is Gary Player of South Africa. He seems to be able to get the ball as near the hole with a five or six iron as most pros do with short irons.

The courses in this country are not particularly long but do have many drive and medium-iron holes; this, naturally, produces many good iron players. They don't go in for great distances with their drives, and so they develop the sort of swing which favours the medium irons—an arc between a three-quarter and full swing.

Most good medium-iron players have the ball roughly in the centre of their feet, and most have about a three-quarter swing, like Scotland's John Panton. Panton is one of the best iron players in Britain, because he doesn't wrap the club round his neck and he has a firm, wristed action which is very smooth.

Five-iron shot: com-table, relaxed position, ll midway between the feet

60   Straight take-away, no wrist-cocking

61   (above left) Wrists now beginning
curl as shoulders and hips turn

62   (above)   Three-quarter backswing,
shoulders and hips fully turned

63   (left)   Knees driving weight forward,
creating late hit

Firm left side, hands and arms delivering the blow

65 *Feet and legs well-positioned, club-head catching up*

66   *Comfortable impact position, head and weight positions steady*

67   *Head still down, club-head and arms completing follow-through*

68   *Poised finish—no tension*

The majority of instruction books pay insufficient attention to medium irons. It seems people take it for granted that if you can hit a drive and a chip you can play these shots, but it is not so. It is important to master the individual techniques of medium-iron play *(59–68)*.

The three-quarter swing is the most important thing; another point of importance is the firm wrist action. The club should be not quite horizontal at the top of the swing. It should still be partly facing the sky and the left wrist must be firm throughout the shot. This keeps the blade of the club square to the target and stops any twists. Although the swing is shorter, this does not mean it's more wristy. One still requires a fairly full turn and a firm position at impact.

Never try and scoop the ball up. This is a very common fault among amateur golfers. If a five iron is used, it has plenty of loft on it and just a normal swing will get the ball airborne. If you try and scoop the ball this will only produce many bad faults such as hitting behind it, topping, and moving the head.

The hands should be level with the ball—never push your hands in front or behind. If you have them behind too much, it will cause scooping, and if you push your hands in front of the ball at the address position your hands will deliver too much of a downward blow and hit the ball too low.

As we are using a shorter swing, it is not necessary to move the left foot as much as with the drive. Accuracy is demanded, and so the less you move your feet the better.

For the stance, although the feet are still roughly shoulder-width apart as with the driver, the left foot should be drawn back from the line slightly, as opposed to the right foot, which is drawn back when driving. The reason for this is that you don't need quite as much turn on the backswing, and having the left foot back a bit will restrict the backswing a little.

With the drive the head should be behind the ball, whereas with the medium iron the head should be almost directly over the ball. As long as the head is over the ball and is kept there, a good accurate shot should be the result.

Knees should always be slightly flexed, a point I recommend for all the strokes.

A calm, unhurried, three-quarter backswing and a

firm sweep with the hands and arms will produce con-sistency with the medium irons providing you have good balance by keeping both feet firmly on the ground.

Always complete the follow-through and make an effort to 'hold' the follow-through. This will help you to achieve good balance and rhythm.

8   How to beat the weather conditions

When the weather is bad the long game is usually affected more than the short. Most club golfers go to pieces in wind and rain but, really, there is no need for this. Just make up your mind you are going to beat the elements. If you follow a few simple procedures there is nothing to be afraid of when the wind blows, or the clouds open.

Rain

One of the most common mistakes made by players who have to play the game in rain is that they try to make up for bad conditions by striving to attain their maximum capability, or even exceed it, on nearly every stroke they play. They speed up the tempo of their whole swing in an effort to hit the ball harder and further, but instead of defeating the handicap they are playing under they usually increase their total considerably when it isn't really necessary.

What you should do when you have to play under bad weather conditions is to exercise restraint and play cautiously and well within yourself. Care should be taken to hit the ball cleanly on all shots rather than the ground behind it.

In taking up your stance make sure that you get a firm footing. It is easy for your feet to slip in wet weather and this can lead to all sorts of problems.

Make sure that you get the ball up in the air. In wet conditions, tee your ball up slightly higher in order to be sure that you will hit it cleanly.

Spend more time over your tee shots. Concentrate on hitting the fairway, even if you have to sacrifice distance in doing it. Playing out of rough with any degree of accuracy or efficiency is almost impossible in wet conditions.

You're obviously not going to get as much distance as you ordinarily do with either your wood clubs or your irons, and, therefore, where you might be inclined to take a four iron under normal conditions, take a three iron to play the same shot when it's wet.

If you have to play a shot from a heavy, close lie, pay special attention to getting it up in the air. Use a shorter-range club, as the ball will float anyway. That is because, in playing the ball out of the wet grass, you're not going to be able to control the spin as well as if you were playing the same shot off dry grass. The ball often flies from a good lie in wet grass.

Take very few chances and don't try to cut corners. Often fairway-wood shots and long-iron shots take an unusual flight off wet ground. Because of that, play for the centre of the green instead of aiming straight for the pin when it is placed in the corner of a green or hidden behind a bunker.

On a wet day, you can discard your brassie and one iron. It is almost impossible to get the correct flight on the ball with such straight-faced clubs.

One essential thing to do when playing golf during wet

weather is to equip oneself for the conditions: umbrellas waterproofs, and towels are three essentials for any golfer on a wet day.

Whatever you do, don't try to keep playing during a thunderstorm. It is best in a really heavy storm to stand out in the middle of the fairway or in a hut. Don't go under a tree. Many of you will remember the tragic death of the Spurs footballer, John White, who was sheltering under a tree on a golf course when he was struck by lightning.

In the early days of my career I would have won a tournament in Ireland if I had been able to play in rain. Since then I have realised that the only way to play in rain is to hit the ball thin. In other words, I find it is better to half-top it along than to take a big divot. The reason for this is that the wet cushions against the ball if you take a divot, and the ball slides off. It produces what is known as a 'flyer'. This must be avoided at all costs when playing in rain. The Ryder Cup men, Neil Coles and Christy O'Connor, are both excellent players in rainy conditions because they nick the ball off the turf without taking a big divot. This is the secret of successful golf in the rain. I have seen many quite good golfers take out wooden clubs and make a big divot; the ball has flown off at all sorts of extraordinary angles because the wet has cushioned between the club and the ball.

Wind

One of the commonest sayings in the golf game is that when the wind blows the men are separated from the boys. To be able to play consistent golf when the wind is blowing is the sign of a good player. It is possible to play good golf in the wind and still control the ball. The idea is to play your shots low into the wind at all times.

Any time you play when the wind is howling—and you will often come up against that on Britain's seaside stretches—remember to widen your stance. Play the ball from a stance in which the ball is back more towards the right foot than you would normally play it.

When addressing the ball, hood the face of your club just a bit and play your hands well in front of the golf club. Concentrate on keeping this at impact.

It is important to make sure you do not pick the club up more abruptly on the backswing or break the wrists early in the swing. For this shot keep your wrists firm.

Remember to hit down and through the ball more sharply than you would on a normal shot, making sure that the hands are leading or drawing the swing and that the weight is well forward on the left foot. Try to keep the club-head as low to the ground as you can on the finish. Try not to let it come up immediately after contact. The hands should still be leading even while you are finishing up on the stroke after contacting the ball.

You will be very interested to see how little a wind will affect a low ball. Of course, when playing in gusty conditions you will have to favour the wind and take advantage of it and make allowances for a certain amount of carry. Just how much carry to allow for, you can usually judge after playing a few strokes. This is another good reason why you should warm up by hitting a few shots before starting a round.

In playing a low shot to a green never try to carry the

green unless it is necessary because of a bunker guarding it. In that case you will have to play a slightly higher shot and make allowance for the wind.

When playing against the wind use a stronger club than you would use for the same distance in still weather. And remember that the ball might well not roll as much when you're playing against the wind and make allowances for it. If you happen to be playing with the wind use a weaker club than you would use under better conditions, and make allowances for the fact that the wind will carry the ball and that you will quite likely get more roll than you ordinarily would on the same stroke in normal conditions.

When the wind is blowing across the line of flight you are planning, take an aim to the right or left of your objective, according to the strength of the wind and its likely affect on that particular shot.

All these points are really common sense, but it's surprising how many club players ignore them when playing in the wind. They start the round in the wrong frame of mind muttering to their friends that the wind will completely ruin their game.

If you follow these simple instructions I have given you will find that golf in the wind can be fun and your scores will be better. Always have confidence in your method and complete the swing without upsetting your usual rhythm.

Personally, I quite like windy conditions because I was brought up in Jersey on a windy course. This is why I like playing the low shots which are needed. I have played them for so long that now I enjoy them; they are second nature to me.

Heat
In Britain, conditions aren't often too hot for golf, but occasionally you get the very hot day and, just like rainy conditions, it is important to follow certain procedures which help your game.

The hottest conditions I have experienced were on the Far East circuit at Bangkok. It was so hot that we were allowed to leave the course at the ninth to go into an air-conditioned room to cool down. Many of the boys almost ran up the ninth hole to get there quickly. I remember that I became very sun-burnt and had to play in a cap and sometimes even had to go out in sunglasses. Heat doesn't affect me too much, luckily, and I don't perspire a lot.

Fortunately, the British climate means that heat does not present too much of a problem here. Just as with rainy conditions, one of the main things to remember is to carry a little towel to rub the grip dry before hitting your shot. The perspiration from your hands gets on your grip and unless you are careful the club will slip.

So whether it rains, blows, or is just steaming hot, you can still enjoy your game, but only if you use your common sense and understand the principles I have outlined in this chapter. Make sure you are properly equipped for these elements and your scores will not rise as the wind and rain do.

9 Club selection

Never underclub—that's the golden rule with regard to club selection. I make a rule now of having a practice round before each event and I never take a club which won't get me past the flag. This way, if I only hit the ball 90 per cent correctly it should still fall near the flag. My perfect shot should go past the flag, the strokes which are not absolutely in the middle of the club but still quite good will be perfect, and the ones which are struck not quite so correctly will still get on the green. That is the only way to play this game. It may sound like common sense, but it is surprising how many players don't think like this.

One of my employers once laughed at me when I told him I took a club which would get me to the back of the green and he said that I was allowing for mishits all the time. My answer to that is that the average professional only hits about half a dozen really perfect shots in a round. Anyhow, I rarely try to hit a flat-out iron shot to the flag.

When I go to a tourney and have a practice round I always ask my caddie in the practice round which club I should take, even though I have made up my own mind. I do this to keep him alert. If you don't ask him in a practice round and you come to the tournament proper and he says, take so and so club, and you think t should be something else, you don't know which way his mind is working, or if he is a good judge. In 1968 I had the same caddie all through the season and it helped because I knew whether he would overclub me or underclub me.

Underclubbing is a very bad fault among amateur golfers. They just don't realise how many strokes this costs them each round. I am sure the average player would improve three or four shots a round if he could guarantee that every shot he hit would be up to the pin or past it.

The club selection for a stroke should always be governed by the amount of loft needed in the flight of the ball and the distance it is to go. The more loft on the club-face, the easier it is to hit a straight ball. The amount of confidence you have in your ability to play a club should be given consideration also, when you are selecting a club to make a shot which appears to be difficult. You can substitute a club you favour for the correct club to be used on a particular shot only if your favourite is quite similar to the correct club in the loft of its club-face.

When you select any club to make a shot, it is well to have an idea of its relation to the distance confronting you. No matter whether they are using woods or irons, no two players will necessarily use exactly the same club for the same distance. The particular range of any club should be adapted to suit the power of the player. Then again, some players tend to loft the ball more easily than other players, in which case, they will use a longer iron to get the same distance as the player who doesn't

69   *This is me driving during the 1965 Esso Tournament at Moor Park. Watching are Max Faulkner (far left) and David Snell*

get as much loft.

The condition of the fairways should also come under consideration. Hard fairways will give you more roll. Soft fairways will stop the ball from rolling.

Next time you go out to practice, pace out how far you hit your wedge, five iron, and driver; then you can, in normal conditions, go by distances marked on tee boxes or cards. If you are reasonably sure of your distance, you will not hurry or force the shot. Select your club and play the shot confidently. If in doubt, stop and change to a club which you know will certainly reach the hole, then there is no need for forcing.

10 Two modern devices which can help your swing

There are two fairly recent innovations which can help [the] player improve his game: they are driving ranges an[d] television. If used properly, both can help you develo[p] a sound swing.

Driving ranges
With the arrival of driving ranges there is ample oppor[-]tunity for all golfers, whether good or bad, to practis[e] their long game. There are ranges near many of th[e] biggest centres in England and they make the unpopula[r] task of practising that much easier.

At most ranges there is ample car-parking space an[d] clubs available for hire. Most are now floodlit, whic[h] means that even on the coldest winter night you can no[w] see your full-blooded wood shot whistle down the range[.] For the beginner who is dedicated to improving hi[s] game, these driving ranges are a blessing. But there ar[e] dangers in driving-range practice, and in this section [I] am going to point one or two of them out to you.

The easiest thing at a range is to buy 60 balls (the[y] usually cost about six shillings) and hit them off in te[n] minutes. Anyone can do this, but unless you know wha[t] you are trying to do little is gained from this exercise.

I spent six months some years ago on a driving range[,] five days a week, just driving balls all the time. For th[e] first two weeks I used to get my 150 balls and I used to slog the ball to see if I could reach the fence in the background. That was good for me as I am small and I needed to get distance. But when I found I could hit it further and reach the fence with a few I decided that now was the time to straighten it up. Then, instead of bashing them all off in 30 minutes, it took me an hour, but I hit 90 per cent more good shots. And it was because I hit the ball better that I became consistently longer. It's easy to hit two out of ten shots 250 yards, but it's hard to average 240 with the whole ten.

People say to me that I seem to be yards longer than I used to be. This is not true. It's just that I now hit more good shots out of the middle of the club and so my average distance has moved up from 200–250 yards to an average of 240.

Too many people buy buckets of balls and smash them away as hard as they can. That is not the important thing. It's far better to hit one shot every two minutes and to think about it and know how you are doing it than to go and hit 60 in ten minutes, which so many people do. That is completely useless and a waste of money. The only thing you will gain if you do this is blisters on your hands.

The other important thing to remember when at the driving range is to make sure you aim your shots at something. Most ranges have targets, but you will find many people just hitting the ball anywhere down the range. Don't do this—always aim at a target.

It is a good idea to keep a little notebook beside you at ranges and write down the number of shots which go to the right and the number which go to the left. This is an excellent way to keep an eye on your progress.

Television

Television has probably played a more important part in bringing about the current boom in golf than any other factor. Many of the people coming into the game first caught the bug when they saw Arnold Palmer or one of the other super-stars in action on television. It looks an easy game when seen on TV, and this helps to give people that urge to go and swing a club.

Tournaments are covered very efficiently, and even the non-golfer can follow what is going on. Live coverage of such events as the US Masters, the US PGA and the Open Championship has, in recent years, been introduced on television. And the intriguing series of matches shown on BBC 2, featuring some of the world's greatest golfers, must have sparked off countless golf careers. Yes, it's the age of television and the question which constantly crops up is 'What are the points to look for when watching the stars on TV?'

There is no doubt in my mind that you can learn much from watching golf on the television, especially when they show the swing in slow motion. I have seen some wonderful shots of Arnold Palmer, Jack Nicklaus, and Gary Player on the BBC 2 series. What I recommend the learner to look for is this wide swing and wide follow-through which I talked about earlier in the book, and the smooth action which nearly all top-class players have. Notice the absence of that jerking which is so often seen during the monthly medal at clubs.

*70　The young South African star, Bobby Cole. I would say that
Bobby must be the longest hitter in the world, pound for pound*

The player who impresses me most when I see him
on TV is the young South African star, Bobby Cole *(70)*.
Bobby has technically one of the best driving actions in

the game. He is so wide and he hits it so far for his size I sometimes find it hard to believe. He does this *only* because of his width of arc and strong arms and supple wrists. I would say that young Bobby must be the longest hitter in the world pound for pound. He weighs less than ten stone. That is the same weight as I am and yet he outdrives me by 30 yards, which is the same distance as big Jack Nicklaus outdrives me by. Next time you have a chance to see Bobby in action make a point of studying his action. It will almost certainly help your own game.